Handbook For Securing Your Home or Small Business Computer Network

3rd Edition

Andrew Meyers

Andrew Meyers

ISBN: 1490908331
ISBN-13: 978-1490908335

Andrew Meyers

CONTENTS

Andrew Meyers

INTRODUCTION

Computer attacks, intrusions and infections have become more infamous among the public due to media coverage. Even electronic warfare between nations has become more prominent and known to the public. The Internet is known to many in the computer security field as the "wild west" and with good reason.

This simple handbook is meant to be a guideline to the fundamentals of computer security within a home or small business environment. When followed properly and maintained, these basics can help to secure computers from most Internet attacks. Simple using only firewalls and anti-virus may not help. You need to employ other techniques that will help protect your computer against threats. This is known as defense-in-depth. If your firewall has holes or your anti-virus software crashed you are vulnerable. Employing the other techniques in this handbook can help secure your network when other mechanisms fail to protect your computer or network.

1

BASICS

This chapter includes three basic computer security steps and an additional one that may not be so well known to casual users. Firewalls, anti-virus, updated software and abstaining from using administrator credentials are all techniques that can go a long way toward protecting your computer.

Firewalls seem to be a well known security device which people are aware of, but unsure of how to use it. In larger, corporate environments, hardware firewalls can be heavily configured. In your home or small business, typically your wireless router acts a hardware firewall by default. All modern operating systems come with a built in software firewall that is fairly efficient.

In Microsoft Windows 10 your firewall should be ON by default, however you can check by doing the following:

1. Use the "Search the web and Windows"

feature at the bottom of the screen.
2. Search for "control panel"
3. When you see "Control Panel" appear at the top of the results, click it.
4. Click "System and Security"
5. Click "Windows Firewall"
6. Click "Turn Windows Firewall on or off" on the left side menu
7. Ensure that the firewall is turned on for both the "Private network settings" and the "Public network settings"

In Mac OS X, you can configure your firewall by doing the following:

1. Click the Apple menu (Apple icon in upper left)
2. Click "System Preferences..."
3. In the top row, click "Security and Privacy"
4. Click the "Firewall" tab
5. Click the "Turn On Firewall" button. If the button is grayed out, click "Click the lock to make changes" option in the lower left of the window and authenticate.

Anti-virus (AV) software is also a well known "must have" for all computers. Many individuals see AV as only necessary on a Windows. **This is absolutely not true.** Many viruses have been written to infect multiple operating systems including Windows, Mac OS X and Linux. This is possible due to vulnerabilities in the Java software which can be

2

installed on any of those operating systems. In June 2013, Java released 40 critical level software patches alone (refer to section below). There are many good **free** AV software solutions for Windows, Mac OS X and Linux.

Free AV software for Windows can be found at the following:

http://www.bitdefender.com/solutions/free.html
https://www.avg.com/en-us/free-antivirus-download

Free AV for Mac OS X:

https://www.avast.com/free-mac-security

Keeping your software up-to-date is a necessity (especially your AV software). Intruders can take advantage of outdated software by exploiting known vulnerabilities before they are fixed. This is similar to a farmer discovering a hole in his fence. He needs to fix it before people start entering his property and stealing his livestock or farm equipment. Software updates come out on a regular basis and many updates can be downloaded and installed automatically via the software's settings. Microsoft releases patches on the second Tuesday of each month. This has become known as "Patch Tuesday".

To update the Windows 10 Operating System follow these steps:

1. Click the Start button
2. Click "Settings"
3. Click "Update & Security"
4. New Windows Updates should download automatically

To update Mac OS X:

1. Click the Apple menu
2. Click "App Store…"
3. Click "Updates" on the top

An important, but largely unknown, technique is to abstain from using an administrator or root account as a primary computer account (the one you use when surfing the web and reading email). When individuals set up their computer for the first time, they typically give themselves administrator privileges. This is bad practice because if the user unwittingly executes malware (malicious software) or clicks a malicious link, the malware will have infected your computer. To correct this, you must give your primary account regular user access. If you need administrator privileges, like installing known good software, in Windows you can simply right click the icon and select "Run as Administrator" (be sure you have set a strong administrator password).

To set your administrator password and give yourself regular User level access in Windows 10:

1. Click the "Start" button
2. Click "Settings"
3. Click "Accounts"
4. Click "Family & other users"
5. Click "Add someone else to this PC"
6. Click "I don't have this person's sign-in information" on the bottom
7. Click "Next?
8. Click "Add a user without a Microsoft account" at the bottom
9. Click "Next
10. Fill out the new user name and password information
11. Click "Next"
12. Click on the new user under the "Other users" section
13. Click "Change Account Type"
14. Click the "Standard User" option under "Account type"
15. Click "OK"

To set your administrator password and give yourself regular User level access in Mac OS X:

1. Click the Apple menu (Apple icon in upper left)
2. Click "System Preferences..."
3. In the fourth row, click "Users & Groups"
4. Set a "Master Password" by click the gear icon

on the left side of the window, under the list of users.

5. Click the "+" button, to the left of the gear icon
6. In the "New Account" drop list, select "Administrator" and continuing filling out the information for the new account. This will be the account you will ONLY use for installing software, changing settings, etc (you can still type in the username/password from your normal account when required)
7. Click the Apple menu
8. Click "Log out *(username)...*"
9. Log in with the newly created administrator account
10. Repeat steps 1 through 3
11. Click on your normal account
12. On the right, for the "Allow user to administer this computer," uncheck the box

2

WEB/EMAIL/GENERAL COMPUTING

The most common uses of a home computer are for browsing the World Wide Web or reading and sending email. Consequently, these are also the most common methods of infection and attack by criminal hackers.

When using a web browser (Internet Explorer, Safari, Chrome, etc) one should consider how well it protects the user from infection and how secure the browser is itself. Although Microsoft Internet Explorer has become more secure over the years it is still not the most secure browser. It is currently ranked #3, far behind Google Chrome and Mozilla Firefox. According to several sources such as PC World Magazine, Lifehacker and Top Ten Reviews, Google Chrome is the most secure web browser (not to mention faster). Chrome has built in auto-updates, malware protection and phishing protection. In addition to these, Google also pays a bounty to anyone who can discover vulnerabilities in the Chrome browser. This helps to secure the software by encouraging discovery, private disclosure and patching of the vulnerability before it can be used maliciously.

To download Google Chrome for any operating system go to:

http://chrome.google.com

Although Google Chrome is already the most secure browser, we can attach other software to it, called extensions, to enhance security.

To view your installed extensions, from within Google Chrome type the following into the address bar at the top:

chrome://extensions

The following extensions can be searched and installed from the following URL:

https://chrome.google.com/webstore/category/extensions

HTTPS Everywhere: Created by the Electronic Freedom Foundation (EFF), this extension will redirect you to a secure connection of any website, if available.
Privacy Badger: Also created by the EFF, this extension blocks tracking software used on websites.
Ghostery: This extension also blocks tracking software used on websites like the extension above.

To block the trackers, make sure they are all selected in the settings. Although this extension has been reported to anonymously send information to advertising agencies, it will still block the trackers from getting to your computer and possibly infecting it.

uBlock Origin: This extension will block advertisements on sites. Besides being annoying, advertisement may sometimes contain malware.

Password Alert: This extension was created by Google and will help you avoid Phishing attacks if you accidentally click on a malicious link.

Flashcontrol: Although unnecessary at this point due to built in protections to Chrome, this plugin gives you more control on whether or not Adobe Flash will play in the browser when a web page loads. If you do download this extension, be sure to download the one "offered by Dave."

Avast Online Security: This extension by the security company Avast, will help avoid Phishing attacks, blocks trackers, and will alert on whether a website is safe or not.

NOTE: These extensions may cause a website to not function properly. If this occurs, simply click the extension's logo in the toolbar of Chrome and disable the extension **ONLY for that website while leaving the extension as a whole enabled.

Chrome has a great feature known as Incognito. When you open an Incognito window in Chrome, cookies, history, session information, PINs, and bank account passwords are not stored or recorded to your hard drive. On certain websites, especially banking websites, the HTTPS protocol (for secure browsing) has been known to store sensitive information onto your hard drive. Using Incognito mode may help to prevent this.

Email is just as ubiquitous as web browsing and therefore an easy path for criminal hackers. There is one simple rule for staying secure with email:

DO NOT *OPEN* ANY SUSPICIOUS EMAILS OR ATTACHMENTS.

This includes people you DO know. Their email may be infected with malware and be using the address list to spread itself to you. If in doubt, contact the person to confirm they sent it.

Phishing is when a criminal hacker tries to gather your username and password to a website, most often a bank. This follows the same rule as above: do not open or respond to these emails. If you do receive an email from your bank, **NEVER CLICK THE LINK IN THE EMAIL.** If you are concerned about your bank account, open Chrome and go directly to the bank's website. You can also call the bank to confirm any issues with your account. Criminal hackers can also masquerade as eBay, Paypal, Amazon or any other service they wish. Be cautious of any emails coming from any institution.

Something that almost everyone has heard of but few people do is to make backup files of your computer. This helps prevent against data loss or infection. A certain type of malware, called ransomware, encrypts your data. To decrypt your data you must pay the criminal hacker money. If you have a backup of your data offsite (outside of your house), you do not have to worry about losing data to ransomware, natural disasters such as fire or a common computer crash.

You can buy unlimited storage, offsite data backup services for less than $60 a year at the following websites:

https://www.backblaze.com/

https://www.carbonite.com

One additional setting is the secure emptying of your Recycle Bin or Trash. Sometimes known as shredding, securely removing files ensures that they cannot be recovered. When a file is emptied from the Recycle Bin or the Trash, the file is not actually gone, only the address for the computer to find the file. This can be compared to an abandoned house. The street address and property may have been reclaimed by the government, but the house is not actually gone until it is destroyed and replaced by another building.

This option has never been available in Windows without a third party software. In newer versions of OS X, the secure delete option has been removed due to the increased use of Solid State Hard Drives. However, in older version of OS X, you can CTRL+click the trash bin.

3

WIRELESS ROUTER SECURITY

Wireless technology is everywhere, especially in our homes. Most home and small business routers sold in stores have built-in wireless networking capability. Because wireless networks are, by default, less secure than wired networks, we must take special care in making sure that our home wireless access points have been secured as best as possible.

First and foremost, we must change the default administration password. The administration password gives access to change any of the router's settings and configuration. This also prevents automated malicious software (known as 'bots') from using your router as part of a worldwide malicious network to attack other computer networks.

**NOTE: The following configurations for this chapter are general directions for the most common models of Linksys and Netgear routers. If your router has a different manufacturer, or you have a different model, use your best judgment when navigating through your routers settings based on the directions below.

To change the administration password on a Cisco Linksys Router:

1. Open Chrome and go to http://192.168.1.1
2. Use the default password of "admin" (without quotes) (no username or "admin" as username)
3. Navigate to "Connectivity" by clicking the "Router Settings" icon (gear icon)
4. Click on the "Basic" tab
5. Next to "Router Password" click "Edit"
6. Type in and confirm a strong password (the strongest passwords are in fact pass-phrases. For example, "The wind is blowing from the north" including the spaces)
7. Hit the "Apply" button and then the "OK" button

To change the administration password on a Netgear router:

1. Open Chrome and go to http://192.168.0.1
2. Use the default password of "password" (without quotes) (use "admin" as username)
3. Click on the "Advanced" tab
4. Click to expand the "Administration" heading
5. Click on "Set Password"
6. Type in the old password, a new strong password and confirm the new password (the

strongest passwords are in fact pass-phrases. For example, "The wind is blowing from the north" including the spaces)

7. Hit the "Apply" button

Because the administration password is so powerful, we also need to make sure that only individuals on your network, and not from the Internet, can log in to and change your router's settings. By default this is usually set but you should check anyway.

To confirm this setting on Cisco Linksys routers:

1. Open Chrome and go to http://192.168.1.1
2. Use the default password of "admin" (without quotes) (no username or "admin" as username)
3. Navigate to "Connectivity" by clicking the "Router Settings" (gear) icon on the left side menu.
4. Click on the "Administration" tab
5. Ensure that the checkbox under the "Remote Access" header is NOT checked

To confirm this option on Netgear routers:

1. Open Chrome and go to http://192.168.0.1
2. Use the administration password and the username "admin"
3. Click the "Advanced" tab at the top
4. Click "Advanced Setup" to expand the section

5. Click "Remote Management"
6. Ensure that the "Turn Remote Management On" at the top is NOT checked

Next, we need to setup or confirm the secure settings of your wireless connection. First and foremost, we need to enable encryption and set a password. Encryption is extremely important, so that criminal hackers cannot see your network traffic. This is one reason why wireless is less secure than a wired network. The criminal hacker has access to your network while sitting in a car across the street, rather than being physically connected by a wire to your network.

To enable wireless encryption and set a password on Cisco Linksys routers:

1. Open Chrome and go to http://192.168.1.1
2. Login with the administration password.
3. Navigate to the "Wireless" settings under "Router Settings" by clicking the Wireless icon on the left side menu.
4. Click on "Edit" to enable encryption (WPA2 Personal) and set a password. You may have two "Edit" buttons to click on and change the settings depending on your model
5. Click "Apply" after making changes and then hit "OK"

To enable wireless encryption and set a password on Netgear routers:

1. Open Chrome and go to http://192.168.0.1
2. Use the administration password and the username "admin"
3. Click the "Basic" tab
4. Click the "Wireless" heading
5. Ensure that the button under "Security Options" is NOT set to "None." AES or TKIP+AES is recommended. There may be more than one "Security Options" header depending on your model router.
6. Hit "Apply" after making changes then hit "OK

While in the wireless configuration page of your router, there are several other options we can change in order to provide additional security. One option is to change the name of your wireless network, also known as a Service Set Identifier (SSID). Criminal hackers tend to target low hanging fruit. Having a default SSID of "linksys" or "netgear" shows that you may have other default settings as well, such as the administration password. Therefore, having a default SSID make you more of a target than your neighbors.

To change your SSID on Cisco Linksys routers:

1. Open Chrome and go to http://192.168.1.1
2. Login with the administration password.
3. Navigate to the "Wireless" settings under "Router Settings" by clicking the Wireless icon on the left side menu.
4. Click on "Edit" to change the "Network Name(SSID)." You may have two "Edit" buttons to click on and change the settings depending on your model
5. Click "Apply" after making changes and then hit "OK"

To change your SSID on Netgear routers:

1. Open Chrome and go to http://192.168.0.1
2. Use the administration password and the username "admin"
3. Click the "Basic" tab
4. Click the "Wireless" heading
5. Change the "Name (SSID)" field. You may have two different fields you need to change depending on your model
6. Hit "Apply" after making changes then hit "OK

Disabling the SSID broadcast is also an option some like to use. Broadcasting your SSID means that when someone searches for wireless networks in the area, your network SSID will show up in a list. For criminal hackers, this is a trivial task to circumvent. Disabling SSID broadcasting will only protect against casual intruders such as lazy or thrifty neighbors.

**NOTE: If you decide to disable SSID broadcasting, you may need to manually enter your SSID on your device every time you need to connect to your wireless router, which can be a nuisance for some.

Unfortunately, the ability to disable the SSID is no longer an available option on newer Cisco Linksys routers.

To disable SSID broadcasting on Netgear routers:

1. Open Chrome and go to http://192.168.0.1
2. Use the administration password and the username "admin"
3. Click the "Basic" tab
4. Click the "Wireless" heading
5. Uncheck the checkbox for "Enable SSID Broadcast." You may have two checkboxes for this option depending on your model
6. Hit "Apply" after making changes then hit "OK

Another option you may want to choose is called MAC filtering. A MAC address is a unique hardware address assigned to every network hardware device, including your computer's wireless card. MAC filtering on a wireless router will allow (or deny) only the MAC addresses you specify to connect to the wireless router. Although this option is also able to be circumvented, it takes more skill to do so than find non-broadcasted SSIDs. This can be useful as a part of defense-in-depth in case other security settings fail. If you do not know how to find the MAC address on all of your other wireless devices (such as smart phone, tablet or e-reader), I would not recommend using this setting.

To enable MAC filtering on Cisco Linksys routers:

1. Open Chrome and go to http://192.168.1.1
2. Login with the administration password.
3. Navigate to the "Wireless" settings under "Router Settings" by clicking the Wireless icon on the left side menu.
4. Click on the "MAC Filtering" tab
5. Click on the button you wish to use. I recommend clicking "Allow access for ONLY the listed MAC Address." You can then get the MAC address for all the devices that are authorized to connect to your network and add them here.
6. Click "Apply" when you are done adding the MAC address then hit "OK"

To enable MAC filtering on Netgear routers:

1. Open Chrome and go to http://192.168.0.1
2. Use the administration password and the username "admin"

3. Click on the "Advanced" tab at the top
4. Click on the "Security" section header
5. Click on "Access Control"
6. Click on the check box labeled "Turn on Access Control"
7. Click on the button you wish to use. I recommend clicking "Block all new devices from connecting." You can then get the MAC address for all the devices that are authorized to connect to your network and add them here.
8. Click "Apply" when you are done adding MAC addresses then click "OK"

One last option that many are not aware of is Wi-Fi Protected Setup (WPS). WPS allows users to easily secure their wireless routers by the touch of a button or just a few clicks. In December of 2011, a flaw in WPS was revealed. Criminal hackers can easily take advantage of this flaw and gain access to your network.

Make sure to update your router's software to the latest version.

4

ENCRYPTION

You have probably heard about encryption in the context of computers and computer security. This is for good reason. Encryption can drastically improve security. You may have heard that when logging into your bank's website to make sure it says "HTTPS" instead of "HTTP." This is because "HTTPS" is encrypted and therefore (generally speaking) cannot be viewed or changed by a criminal hacker. Encryption is even more important on portable devices such as laptops, smart phones and tablets. These devices most likely contain personal information, or at least session information for websites including your bank (For more on this, refer to previous section on Chrome's Incognito mode). Windows and Mac OS X have whole disk encryption which will encrypt your entire hard drive. In the case you lose or have your laptop/phone/tablet stolen, the whole disk encryption will prevent others from accessing your personal information.

Built-in whole disk encryption (BitLocker) is only available on Pro, Enterprise and Education versions of Windows 10. It is not available on the Home edition of Windows 10. VeraCrypt (discussed below) is a free alternative for other versions.

To enable BitLocker:

1. Use the "Search the web and Windows" feature at the bottom of the screen.
2. Search for "control panel"
3. When you see "Control Panel" appear at the top of the results, click it.
4. Click "System and Security"
5. Click "BitLocker Drive Encryption"
6. Click "Turn on BitLocker" next to the drive you want to encrypt, most likely C:\
7. For the "Use a password to unlock the drive", check the box
8. Enter and confirm a strong password or passphrase
9. Click the "Next" button
10. Click "Save the recovery key to a USB flash drive" (You can select the other options, but make sure you save the recovery key on media OTHER than the drive you are encrypting)
11. Click "Yes" to acknowledge the warning
12. Click the "Next" button
13. Click "Start Encrypting"

To enable whole disk encryption (FileVault) in Mac OS X:

1. Click the Apple menu
2. Click "System Preferences..."
3. In the top row, click "Security and Privacy"
4. Click the "FileVault" tab
5. Click on the "Turn on FileVault" button. If the button is grayed out, click on the "Click the lock to make changes" option in the lower left of the window and authenticate.
6. Copy the Recovery Key to a safe place.
7. Choose your option to store your Recovery Key with Apple or not.
8. Click "Restart" to begin the encryption process

Third-party software that is also capable of doing whole disk encryption is VeraCrypt. VeraCrypt is free, open source software with many features. Aside from whole disk encryption, VeraCrypt also has the ability to create a hidden encrypted drive. This drive appears as a normal file on your computer and you load it whenever you need to access it. This is a great place to store files with personal information on them, such as taxes, copy of passports, etc.

You can download VeraCrypt from:

https://www.veracrypt.fr

With the ubiquitous usage of passwords for almost every website you visit, many people find it difficult to remember all of these passwords. Because of this many individuals re-use passwords. This is extremely bad practice. If one website is compromised, an attacker now knows your username/password for numerous other websites as well.

To help fix this dilemma, online password managers have come to the rescue with the best being LastPass. You can sign up for a free account at https://www.lastpass.com. Online password managers, such as LastPass, allow you to randomize passwords for all websites you visit while leaving you to remember only one master password. If a website you use is compromised, LastPass will alert you and in some cases, change the password for you.

When I tell people that I use LastPass, the most popular question is, "What if LastPass is compromised?" LastPass only stores your passwords with a strong encryption. All the encryption/decryption is done when you use a password on a website. This means that if LastPass is compromised, at most the attacker will only be able to get encrypted passwords which would take centuries to crack.

In addition to LastPass helping manage passwords, it also helps defend against phishing attacks. LastPass automatically recognizes websites for which you have an account. If you visit a website for which you do not have an account, the LastPass icon will not be present.

I've mentioned previously that by using the Internet without encryption, criminal hackers can view the information you are viewing, including emails. Many times, when traveling, you may connect to a public wireless access point. Even when paying for wireless access, that doesn't mean the connection you are using, is encrypted. If the connection is unencrypted, you are vulnerable to eavesdropping. This is where a Virtual Private Network (VPN) comes in handy. VPN software creates a secure tunnel through the public wireless access point. This can be compared to using an armored truck. The material inside the armored truck is safe while traveling through the mean streets of the Internet. Using a VPN is highly encouraged by many in the computer security community whenever you connect to an un-trusted network, including laptops, phones and tablets.

You can download VPN software from:

https://www.vpnsecure.me

5

ADDITIONAL SECURITY CONFIGURATIONS

These additional settings are something a regular user is usually unaware of but can be extremely useful. The computer warning that advanced settings should only be adjusted by experts tends to scare away most people. However, some of these settings can be extremely useful. Some of these configurations are the same that are used (or should be) on a corporate network only implemented differently due to the size of the environment.

The simplest of these settings is to enable the feature to display the extension type of file names. This means that, on Microsoft Windows, instead of seeing "installer" you would see "installer.exe." The extension .EXE is an executable file for Microsoft Windows which would install or run a program. The benefit of doing this is that you can determine what type of file you are about to select and open. Many criminal hackers take advantage of this by naming their malware "ImportantDocument.doc.exe" which is an executable program. However, if you did not have the "View file extensions" option enabled, you would only see the file as "ImportantDocument.doc" which would only look like a simple benign Microsoft Word document, not an executable file. Criminal hackers prey on this option not being enabled and the user's naivety of file extensions.

To enable file extensions in Microsoft Windows 10:

1. Use the "Search the web and Windows" feature at the bottom of the screen.
2. Search for "control panel"
3. When you see "Control Panel" appear at the top of the results, click it.
1. Click "Appearance and Personalization"
2. Click "File Explorer Options"
3. Click the "View" tab, and then, under "Advanced settings", uncheck the "Hide extensions for known file types" check box
4. Click "OK"

To enable file extensions in Mac OS X:

1. Click the Finder icon in the Dock
2. In the Menu bar at the top of the screen, click "Finder"
3. Click "Preferences..."
4. Click "Advanced"
5. For the option "Show all filename extensions," check the box

The next security configuration can help increase your security; however it can also render some websites that you visit inoperable. Luckily, Chrome has options to help. JavaScript is a computer language that programmers use to create features on websites. However, since JavaScript is highly configurable, it can also be used to compromise computers. You can disable JavaScript in the Chrome web browser (and Java and ActiveX in Internet Explorer) through the settings. Chrome also lets you add exceptions for websites you know are not malicious, so that JavaScript is no longer blocked on the sites you specify.

To disable JavaScript on Chrome:

1. Click the "Customize and Control" button in the upper right of the browser windows. This icon resembles 3 stacked horizontal lines.
2. Click "Settings." This will open a new browser tab with the settings.
3. Click "Advanced" at the very bottom of the page
4. Under the "Privacy and security" heading, click the "Content settings..." button
5. Under the "JavaScript" heading select "Do not allow any site to run JavaScript"

**NOTE: Additionally, you can add the websites you know are not malicious and need JavaScript to run (facebook.com, etc) in this window. You can also add websites "on the fly" by going to the website. Whenever you visit a website and Java is blocked, a scroll icon with a red X will appear on the right of the address bar. If you trust this website and want to add it to your exception, click this icon and add the website to the exceptions.

Almost everyone who is a computer user, especially in the business world, is familiar with Adobe PDF files. PDF files, like Microsoft Word documents, can be used to deliver malicious content (viruses, malware, etc) to your computer. Hidden code within the PDF file can execute when you open a PDF document. This is one example of why you should never open attachments from suspicious emails. However, in line with defense-in-depth, we can employ software configurations to protect us in the event we open a PDF file that contains malware. One such configuration is called a sandbox. A sandbox provides protection from malicious code by containing the code within pre-defined borders; this will prevent it from interacting with any other software including the operating system.

A free PDF reader with sandbox capabilities for Microsoft Windows can be downloaded from:

http://www.foxitsoftware.com/Secure_PDF_Reader

Although FoxIt Secure PDF Reader is recommended over Adobe PDF Reader, FoxIt Software does not currently make a Secure PDF Viewer for Mac OS X.

When using Adobe PDF Reader for Mac OS X, make sure the "Protected Mode" is enabled in Preferences.

The Domain Name System (DNS) is an Internet protocol responsible for translating names such as "google.com" to a machine readable IP address like "173.194.34.32." This service is necessary so you don't have to remember these blocks of numbers to all your favorite websites. The DNS system can be compared to the mailing address system. When you want to go to a friend's house, you tell your spouse you are going to "Mike's house" not that you are going to "1234 Main St." "Mike's house" gives more information and is easier to remember than all of your friend's home addresses.

The DNS system is used by malware on an infected machine to communicate back to a control server. This server then controls the malware and may use your computer for computer crimes, steal your credit card information, bank accounts or passwords. Because the malware uses DNS to communicate, we can use DNS to prevent this communication from happening. If the DNS name for the malware control server or a website that spreads malware is known, we can adjust the DNS settings to protect your computer.

The DNS provider OpenDNS does just this. If a malicious server or website is found, OpenDNS changes its configuration files so that the computers that use its service are not infected. To sign up for a free OpenDNS account please visit https://www.opendns.com. With an OpenDNS account you can use features similar to a corporate network. This includes Web Content Filtering.   Web Content Filtering can block certain types of websites such as Gambling, Parked Domains, Adware and Web Spam. (These are the categories that I recommend be additionally blocked for security reasons).

In addition to   Web Content Filtering, OpenDNS also provides the ability to block individual domains. This can include top-level domains (TLD)   such as ".com" or country-level domains such as ".co.uk".

The country-level domains I recommend be blocked are as follows:

ru
cn
ng
ro
br
ua
gq

Besides the United States, the most malicious activity comes from China (cn) and Russia (ru) followed by Brazil (br). The others, Nigeria (ng), Romania (ro), Equatorial Guinea (gq) and the Ukraine (ua) are also known for suspicious activity. It's a good idea to block these domains even if you don't think you will visit a website located in this country. Malware often needs to contact servers in these countries to continue installation of their malicious software.

I also recommend adding the following top-level domains. These domains have been discovered to house over 97% malicious domains within their respective TLDs:

.country
.cricket
.kim
.link
.party
.review
.science
.work
.zip

After creating an account, to use OpenDNS you simply need to enter the OpenDNS server IP addresses on your Internet router.

The current IP addresses for OpenDNS can be found here:

https://www.opendns.com/opendns-ip-addresses

To change the DNS settings on a Cisco Linksys router:

1. Open Chrome and go to http://192.168.1.1
2. Use the default password of "admin" (without quotes) (no username or "admin" as username)
3. Navigate to "Connectivity" by clicking the "Router Settings" (gear) icon on the left side menu.

4. Click on the "Internet Settings" tab
5. Click "Edit" next to the "Type of Internet Connection" header
6. Change the "DNS 1" and "DNS 2" options to the IP addresses you can find using the OpenDNS URL above.

To change the DNS settings on a Netgear router:

1. Open Chrome and go to http://192.168.0.1
2. Use the administration password and the username "admin"
3. Click the "Basic" tab at the top
4. Click the "Internet" icon in the center of the page
5. Under the header "Domain Name Server (DNS) Address, click the option for "Use These DNS Servers"
6. Enter the IP address you found on the OpenDNS URL above into the "Primary DNS" field and "Secondary DNS" field
7. Click "Apply" when you are done and then click "OK"

If you are unable to add the OpenDNS IP addresses to your router, you can also configure your computer to use the OpenDNS servers, although configuring your router is the preferred and more secure method.

To set your DNS settings in Microsoft Windows 10:

1. Use the "Search the web and Windows"

feature at the bottom of the screen.

2. Search for "control panel"
3. When you see "Control Panel" appear at the top of the results, click it.
4. Click "Network and Internet"
5. Click "Network and Sharing Center"
6. On the left, click "Change adapter settings"
7. Double-click the adapter you wish to change, most likely labeled "Local Area Connection"
8. Click the "Properties" button
9. Highlight "Internet Protocol Version 4 (TCP/IPv4)" and click the "Properties" button
10. On the bottom, select "Use the following DNS server addresses:"
11. Enter the IP address found from the OpenDNS URL found above

To set your DNS settings in Mac OS X:

1. Click the Apple menu
2. Click "System Preferences..."
3. In the third row, click "Network"
4. Click the "Click the lock to make changes" option in the lower left of the window and authenticate.
5. Click your main network adapter on the left. Your main network adapter should have a green circle to the left of it
6. On the lower right side, click the "Advanced" button
7. Click the "DNS" tab
8. Click the "+" on the lower left side of the

window, under the "DNS Servers" heading
9. Enter the IP addresses found from the OpenDNS URL found above

Before a DNS name is resolved to an IP address using Internet DNS servers, it first looks to a file called "hosts" which is present on all computer systems. The "hosts" file is a simple text file that lists a DNS name next to its IP address. This file is used first because it is faster to check than to check with your closest DNS server on the Internet. We can change this file so that known malicious websites are automatically blocked. You may be thinking that OpenDNS will take care of this problem, but we want to continue our use of a defense-in-depth strategy. If OpenDNS hasn't configured their settings to block a website that you know is bad, your "hosts" file will protect you.

You can get the updated malware domain list from:

http://www.malwaredomainlist.com/hostslist/hosts.txt

**NOTE: If you are a more advanced user, or like to explore, I personally use OpenWRT custom firmware on my wireless Internet router. Since this firmware is based on Linux, it has a "hosts" file. I put my configuration in this file on the router so I don't have to update all of my computers.

To edit your "hosts" file in Microsoft Windows:

1. Click the Start button
2. Click "File Explorer"
3. Navigate to the following location C:\Windows\System32\drivers\etc
4. Double-click the "hosts" file (not "hosts.txt", if it exists)
5. In the "Open with" window, select "Notepad" (if "Notepad" doesn't show, click the "Browse" button and navigate to C:\Windows. Select "notepad.exe" and click the "Open" button
6. Click "OK"
7. Below the comments, paste all the text from the file from the URL above. Be sure that the "hosts" file saves without an extension. Often, the Notepad program wants to save the file with a .txt extension. If you see this after saving, rename the file and just remove the .txt extension.

To edit your "hosts" file in Mac OS X:

1. Click the Apple menu
2. Click "Log Out (username)..."
3. Log in with the administrator account
4. Click the magnifying glass icon in the upper right, next to the clock
5. Type "terminal" (without the quotes) and hit Enter

6. In the window that pops up, type "sudo defaults write com.apple.Finder AppleShowAllFiles TRUE && killall Finder" (all on one line, without the quotes) and hit Enter
7. Click the Finder icon in the Dock
8. In the Menu bar at the top of the screen, click "Finder"
9. Click "Preferences..."
10. Click "Sidebar"
11. Under the "Devices" heading, make sure the option "Hard disks" has a check mark and not a "-"
12. Click the Red Circle in the upper left of the window to close it
13. Click the Finder icon in the Dock to open a Finder window
14. On the left hand side, under the "DEVICES" heading, click "Macintosh"
15. Double-click the "etc" folder
16. Double-click the "hosts" file
17. Below the text, paste all the text from the file from the URL above

In addition to blocking known malicious sites, you can also block advertisements, which may redirect you to a malicious site. You can use the above steps to edit your "hosts" file and add these settings onto the end of your "hosts" file.

The updated list of advertising DNS names are found here:

http://www.winhelp2002.mvps.org/hosts.txt

To add these entries to your "hosts" file, follow the steps above for your operating system and paste the advertising domains below the malware domains in the "hosts" file. Also, as new malware domains and advertising domains are created every day, remember to stay up to date with your "hosts" file by using the information from the provided URLs.

For those individuals advanced enough, blocking entire countries can be a great advantage to a defensive strategy. If you have no need for traffic going to/from countries such as China, Russia and Brazil you can deny that traffic in several ways. The following website offers all IP addresses located in a certain country. It is provided in several formats such as IP Tables (a popular command line firewall for Linux and Unix), Cisco router Access Control Lists (ACL), and Apache .htaccess files.

https://www.ip2location.com/blockvisitorsbycountry.aspx

As mentioned above in the OpenDNS section, I recommend blocking the following countries, in order of importance:

China
Russia
Brazil
Ukraine
Romania
Nigeria
Equatorial Guinea

Remember it's a good idea to block these IP addresses even if you don't think you will visit a website located in this country. Malware infections often need to contact servers in these countries to continue installation of their malicious software.

As stated in the Introduction, security best practice is employ a defense-in-depth strategy. That is, using multiple control mechanisms to defend against a single known threat. The advantage to this is that if one control fails or is bypassed, the other will block it.

A great addition to any home or small business network is a Unified Threat Manager (UTM). Sophos offers software that can help protect your entire network at a single point rather than on every single device. You need to you use your own hardware to install the software, so I recommend only advanced users attempt this.

You can find the software at the link below:

https://www.sophos.com/en-us/products/free-tools/sophos-utm-home-edition.aspx

ABOUT THE AUTHOR

Andrew Meyers has a Master's Degree in Information Security from a prominent university and several high level information security certifications. He also has experience in information collection while serving in Iraq with U.S. Special Operations.